# IF FREUD WERE A GOLFER

Dr. Roy Ehrlich
Dr. Marijanet Doonan

Peterboro Press
2026

**ISBN 978-0-9847094-3-4**

# DEDICATION

**To Roy,** my North Star, who loved life and helped others to do the same. He enjoyed golf and, as a Psychiatrist, liked writing about what Freud would have thought about golf.

**To Ryan Jenkins**, our long-time editor, who sent us a case of wine after editing this book.

**To the Publishers at Peterboro Press**,who laughed a good deal as they read this submission and decided to publish it to have golfers think about Freud as they played the game.

**To our friends and neighbors** who golfed over the years and remained friends after they read this book.

**To our children,** who tolerated our sense of humor but thought we should have considered using pseudonyms as authors.

In this Book, you will learn about the game of golf as it might have been interpreted by the famous Psychiatrist Sigmund Freud.

As you play your game of golf, enjoy Freud's possible interpretations of various aspects of this game of champions.

# If Freud Were a Golfer

If Freud were a golfer, he would most certainly have analyzed the game as he had most of life. As an avid anti-feminist, he would have heartily approved of the acronym from which we derive the name *G O L F*, which stands for

*Gentlemen Only Ladies Forbidden.*

If we look psychoanalytically at the activity we call golf, we are instantly struck by the fact that it is an allegory for masculinity. To start, there is the *driver*, a significant club used in this activity. There is great pride expressed about the nature of the club, its length, and the size of the head. Also included with the driver is the *head cover*. Often, the *head cover* portrays an animal, a tiger, a bear, or another aggressive creature, all meant to advertise the masculinity of the possessor.

The next piece of equipment that has significant sexual overtones is the *ball.* Not only does the expression *ball power* and *having balls* blatantly express the macho image, but the name given by the manufacturer to balls further enhances this symbolism. We have the god *Nike* and the supreme *Titlest,* as well as *Pro Staff* and other similar illusions to penile supremacy. The older population and those with erectile dysfunction are not left out of the picture, hence we have the *Noodle.* So, no matter where the male stands in the hierarchy of penile grandeur, some ball will represent him. Even the psychiatrically challenged are represented by the *Loco*.

The clubs, the balls, and all the other paraphernalia are placed in a *golf bag*.

Generally, in keeping with the need to prove masculinity, the bag is large and ornate with many endorsements. Of course, the best bags are made of skin — read “leather” — or some synthetic made to look like leather. Hence the scrotal symbolism.

If we delve further into the unconscious, we must look at the golf activity itself. To start, the individual strides proudly to his scrotal symbol, *his bag*, and pulls out his *club* and takes off the *head cover* to reveal the head in all its glory.

Then, he strides to a display area called the *tee box.* There, he reaches into his pants and pulls out a *ball,* which he places with great care upon a special pedestal, called a *tee,* for all to admire.

Next, he stands over this symbol of his masculinity for some time, pointing with his club at his ball. This is called *addressing the ball.* In so doing, he is certain that all will see his shiny, recently cleansed ball.

In case anyone missed the display, he takes his club and points back and forth at the ball. This is politely called the *waggle*. But we all know it is a way to call attention to not only the ball but what is to follow, the actual stroking of the ball. Once he does this, he then hits his ball.

Once the person is sure that all have observed his ball and club, and that a devout hush has fallen over his group, he proceeds to demonstrate his testosterone level by hitting the ball as far as he can. Note that although some lip service is given towards hitting the ball in a straight line, all understand that distance, and therefore power, is the ultimate criterion. Next, the other members of the group try to outdo him and each other to prove who is the most manly.

Eventually, the ball comes to rest on the flat, lush, “short stuff,” called the *green*. The object here is to get the ball in the *hole*. We don’t think elaboration is necessary here about the very obvious sexual meaning of that concept.

To further illustrate that this is a demonstration of male sexual power, the quicker you get in the hole, with the fewest strokes, the better. As an aside, we could look at the issue of strokes, as in masturbation, and write a whole additional treatise especially for those who would rather play the “game” alone.

But, back to the fewest strokes. The absolute height of golfing pleasure is when the golfer can skip all the foreplay and get the ball in the hole in one shot. This is taken as the crowning glory of golfing masculinity, even though we all know it is almost entirely an accident.

However, remember that Freud said there are no accidents, and all is controlled by the unconscious.

A degree of sexual hostility is expressed by just stepping up and putting your ball in the hole without any preamble or foreplay. We have yet to see a golfer kiss his ball prior to hitting it.

18
MORE
HOLES

Men take this testosterone display, "The Game of Golf," very seriously. For many, the aspect of competitiveness is very strong. Men strive mightily to win and therefore prove themselves.

People of advanced age, often with significant career accomplishments in their lives, still need to win. Some go out daily and play eighteen or thirty-six or even more holes to prove themselves and to increase their prowess.

Typical of the insecurity that exists in men about their sexuality, many times there is cheating involved, and often arguments occur about insignificant details. So important is the outcome of the game that there is often substantial betting on the results. There is even a gambling game called *skins*, possibly shortened from foreskins.

Even though the most obvious aspect of golf is proving masculinity, there is also the homosexual aspect. Generally, men get together to "*play*." They go into a locker room and undress in front of each other. and often shower in a community shower. Afterwards, they sit around drinking and regaling each other with their exploits.

The psychoanalytic hour would not be complete if we didn't examine the unconscious symbolism of golf for women. As Freud said, nothing is done without some unconscious meaning.

As we have explained, the game of golf is meant as a determinant of masculine prowess; therefore, the only psychoanalytical conclusion that makes sense is that women play golf because of penis envy. They go through the same rituals as do the men and have essentially the same goal.

That is, to prove how masculine they are. The only other possible interpretation is a Lorena Bobbitt complex in that they wish to hit and destroy these male symbols.

A CIGAR
IS JUST
A CIGAR
GOLF
IS JUST
A GAME

The next time you run into golfers and they talk about their round of golf, remember the psychoanalytical overtones. You may understand golfers better and have extra insight into what they are really saying.

Finally, a word of caution. Since we are using Freudian theory as our guideline, we must remember one of Freud's more insightful observations.

"Sometimes a cigar is just a cigar!"
"Golf is just a game!"

## About The Authors

"**Dr. Roy Ehrlich** enjoyed playing golf since childhood. Roy had four "holes in one" in his lifetime. He said it was because he was a lucky and relaxed golfer. As a psychiatrist, he decided it would be interesting to write about what Freud would have said about golf. He did agree that Freud'sthoughts may have gone beyond just playing a game."

"**Dr. Marijanet Doonan** was not a golfer; she played tennis. She admitted she did play golf - badly - with Roy a few times. She thought a book about Freud would be fun, but Freud's thoughts might have been a bit "way out there" about golf. She said many of her female friends enjoyed golf as a game."

"I asked them both if they spoke with their patients about golf, and both replied, Rarely."

Ryan Jenkins, Editor

www.ingramcontent.com/pod-product-compliance
Lightning Source LLC
LaVergne TN
LVHW010842120826
845149LV00020B/3490

*9780984709434*